*t i m   a b b o t*

first published in great britain in 1996 by
pavilion books limited
26 upper ground, london se1 9pd

text copyright © tim abbot 1996
photographs copyright © tim abbot 1996
cover shot © pat pope 1996
pages 40 & 41 © michael spencer jones 1996
pages 96 & 97 © nellee hooper 1996

designed by josh eve and damian hale
project coordination by leesa daniels

a CIP catalogue record for this book is available from the british library

ISBN 1 85793 862 3 (hbk)

ISBN 1 86205 045 7 (pbk)

typeset in helvetica 12pt
printed and bound in spain by bookprint

2 4 6 8 10 9 7 5 3 1

this book may be ordered by post direct from the publisher
please contact the marketing department
but try your bookshop first.

goodsexbaddrugsuglyrock'n'roll

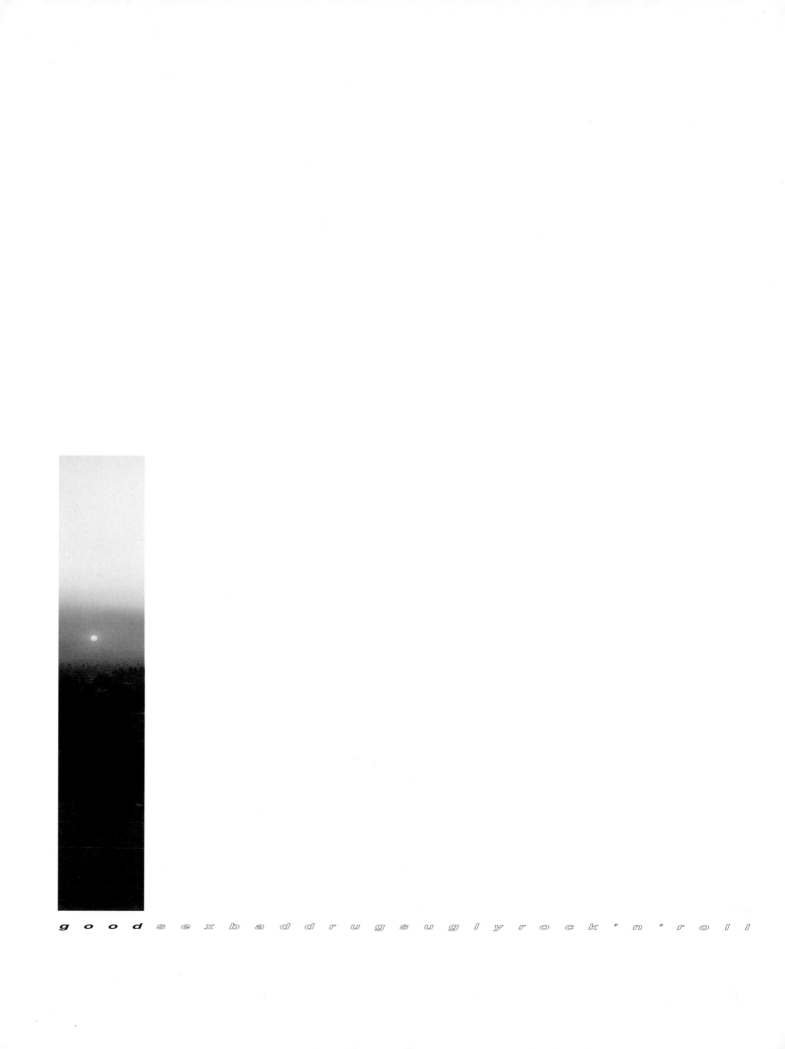

*good* s e x b a d d r u g s u g l y r o c k ' n ' r o l l

fourwords

'your time has come'
noel gallagher, 1996

'who are the abbots?'
liam gallagher, 1996

*Noel Gallagher.*          *Liam Gallagher*

'a book without pictures is a shit book'
liam gallagher, dublin 1996

to 'our mams'

mum and dad,
liam, noel, bonehead,
guigs and alan

and to the two chris's in my life
christine wanless and chris abbot

live forever

creation records was a ritualistic and strange, uncompromising culture. the ramshackle offices had withstood yet another ecstasy and jack daniels impromptu party. the company, which comprised various misfit geniuses, was well versed in abuse and the ceremony of trashing the office at 5am, then re-opening at 10am for business. this party had not been significant by normal standards, bar the words NORTHERN IGNORANCE which had been scrawled in black marker pen across the reception's ceiling. the day after this extravaganza noel and liam gallagher came in and said that this label (particularly the ceiling) felt like home.

in 1993/94 the music of the world was the seattle/generation x/grunge/wall of sound. the US influence in rock was domineering. the UK could only answer back with the limp-wristed mutterings of brett and his suedettes. it's easy to say you're the greatest rock 'n' roll band (cocaine has never been the truth drug of choice), however, one day you have to substantiate it.

the bunker was the ground-floor office which alan mcgee, dick green and myself shared. we used to go though the overdrafts of alan's audio-visionary art statements. this entrepreneurial alliance never made hardcore money yet it was the last bastion of true independent music. music over money.

on the desk was the cassette box which stood out from the bin liner of other hopefuls. on the box was a twisted spiral of the union jack with OASIS blocked out of the middle. liam commented, 'yeah, man! this is the greatest flag in the world and it's just going down the toilet. we are going to be the biggest band in the world. we're british and it's just rock 'n' roll!' liam paced up and down the office like a caged leopard. noel ignored his brother's rants and got serious. he knew that creation was the right label, the right people, but it wasn't about money or the general music-business bollocks — it was about do you

# BELIEVE?

soon to become ashen-faced youth and not so youth — not a dry eye in the house. sign on the dotted line ................................................................................ said a corporate type.

good**sex**baddrugsuglyrock'n'roll

back from a holiday in
portugal, in the comfort of
his mum's back garden,
the kid pulls the cover off
a vintage '55 lambretta.
bought a couple of years
before for nothing, this is
the kid's pride and joy
and it means everything.

sticks and stoned could break your
bones but guigs will never
shake you

white here! white now!
cute, cheeky, chirpy, cockney
drummer chappy alan white gives
it large backstage at earls court.

*earls court, november '95*

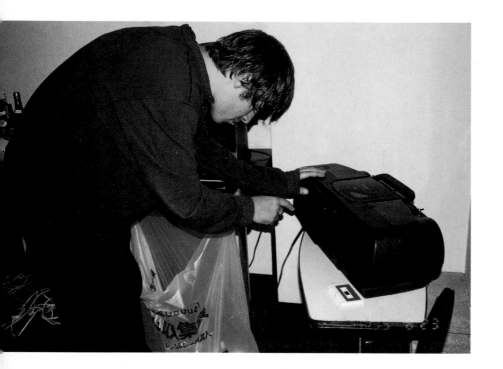

after just completing the last of five tokyo dates, the band chill out and relax in the dressing room.
oasismania had swept through japan and the fans' welcome had been outstanding.
taking it all in, the kid refreshes himself and takes control of the stereo. what did he play?
oasis.
who else?

liquid room, tokyo, september '95

**happiness is a grape called gallagher**

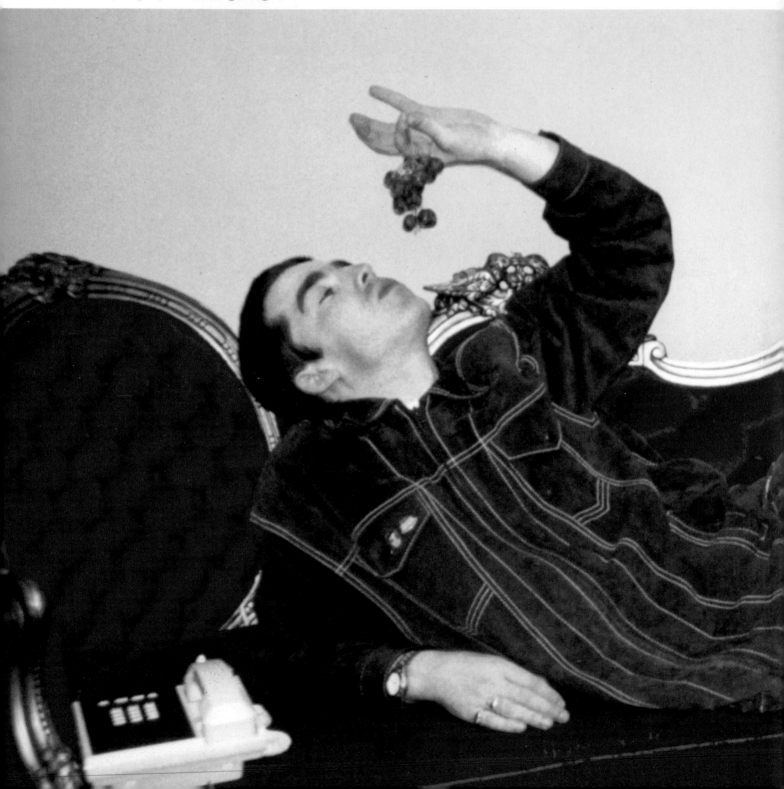

after all...you're

'5 PLUS

9                    9A                    10

long time love is all you need.